Document Shredding Museum

Publication of this book was made possible, in part, with assistance from the LitRI Translation Funding Program of the National Book Committee and the National Agency for Language Development and Books, Ministry of Education and Culture of the Republic of Indonesia.

First published 2019 by Reading Sideways Press
20 Tennyson Street, Richmond, VIC, 3121

readingsidewayspress.com
readingsidewayspress@gmail.com

This book is copyright. The copyright of the original text belongs to Afrizal Malna. The copyright of the translation belongs to Daniel Owen. Except for private study, research, criticism or reviews, as permitted under the Copyright Act, no part of this book may be reproduced, stored in a retrieval system, or transmitted in any form or by any means without prior written permission. Enquiries should be made to the publisher.

The cover design is based on Afrizal Malna's poem, "Workshop 2: Duration Editing" (p.26). The title of the original poem is "Workshop 2: Editing Durasi" Afrizal Malna, museum penghancur dokumen, Yogyakarta: Garudhawaca, 2013, p.19.

Typeset in Caudex

National Library of Australia
Cataloguing-in-publication data is available at http://catalogue.nla.gov.au

ISBN 978-0-6482610-7-0

Document Shredding Museum

Museum Penghancur Dokumen

CONTENTS

Shadow Bridge: Translating Afrizal Malna's *Museum Penghancur Dokumen*   09

Part 1 – Under the Word Ruler   13

- Eraser's Guest   14
- Used Language Shops A and B   15
- Photography Gallery   17
- Sharp Prison   18
- Dragonfly Above a Tall Fence   19
- 16th Floor Music   20
- Techniques to Entertain the Viewer   21
- Nail Holes   22
- December's Ruler   23
- There's No Meaning: A Repeating Poem   25
    - *Workshop 1: Portrait Diagram*   25
    - *Workshop 2: Duration Editing*   26
    - *Workshop 3: To See*   27
    - *Workshop 4: To Look*   28
    - *Workshop 5: My Captive*   29

Part 2 – Archive Shadows   31

- Poetry Seminar at the Sunda Strait   32
    for Goenawan Mohamad
- Not About Being Broken   36
    (a bridge from Murtidjono)
- Document Shredding Machine   38
- Betel Chalk Blast Process   39
- Spice Bridge   41
- Fire in a Briefcase   42
- For Sir Life   43
- A Policy Proposal for the Police   44

Activities of Ice Blocks	46
Rock in a Shoe	47
Don't Forget the Shallots	49
Winter Seminar	52
Chinese ID Card	53
for Lan Zhenghui	
New Order Architecture in Your Home	55
Under Gatoloco's Gamelan	57
Cryptic News from Darmo Gandul	59
Seminar on Lunto Kloof	60
Last Station Stop	61
for Slamet Gundono	
Raincoat in Two Cities	63
Clapping Behind a Fence	65
for Cahyo, the guitarist who always plays from his tears	
Merapi Dinner	67
Ears of Revolution	69
Birthday with Wianta	70
The Hudoq Dance of Matalibaq	71

Part 3 – Voices that Walk on Glass   73

Voices that Walk on Glass	74
The Project of Aborting Me	76
Dead Man Epidemic	78
A Street to Fall On	79
Museum of Poems From the Missing	80
Portrait of a Felled Tree	82
Strategy on a Chair	83
Loneliness on the 5th Floor of a Hospital	84
Sermon Beneath an Electric Pole	86
The Secret of the Leak	87
A Sea for Fitri	88

In Line for Money at the Bank	90
Gloomy Sunday	91
Across from a Leaf	92
Luring Seven Butterflies	93
Lublinskie's Body in a Black Ice Alleyway	94
for Gas	
Wind Beneath an Ear	96
Guest of a Time	98
Index	99
Afterword: Notes Beneath Shadows	100
Acknowledgments	109
About Afrizal Malna	110
About Daniel Owen	111
About Reading Sideways Press	112

SHADOW BRIDGE: Daniel Owen
Translating
Afrizal Malna's
*Museum Penghancur
Dokumen*

*How could poetry enable us to walk
with our own shadow, through our selves
still asleep on a train.*
— Afrizal Malna,
"Poetry Seminar at the Sunda Strait"

I first met Afrizal Malna in October 2017, at Kampung Buku Jogja, an annual literary event with a book fair, readings, and discussions held on the grounds of Universitas Gadjah Mada in Yogyakarta. I had just come to stay awhile in Jogja, to study Indonesian language and literature. While my Indonesian was passable when we met, I hadn't yet read much contemporary writing and was quite ignorant of the literary landscape. Afrizal and I were introduced by mutual friends following his discussion of theater and poetry with Gunawan Maryanto. I picked up a copy of his book of short stories, *Pagi Yang Miring Ke Kanan* (*A Morning Slanting to the Right*), newly published at the time by Penerbit Nyala, and we chatted briefly.

Following our initial meeting, I started reading Afrizal's work and quickly found myself falling into its rabbit hole. His poetic sensibility felt familiar, yet at the same time revelatory; I felt a tickling of the senses both troubling and pleasurable. It was the kind of reading experience that takes you outside of yourself while making you feel more yourself. I came to learn that Afrizal is generally regarded as an important but inscrutable innovator in the Indonesian poetic tradition. In addition to his work as a poet, he has been involved with visual and performance art, long active as a theater-maker, playwright, artist, novelist, and critic. Since the early 1980's, his literary work has been widely published and respected, and has even given rise to the literary critical term "Afrizalian." His work has won a number of national and international literary honors, notably the SEA Write Award for *Teman-Temanku Dari Atap Bahasa* (*My Friends from the Roof of Language*) and the Khatulistiwa Literary Award for *Museum Penghancur Dokumen* (*Document Shredding Museum*), and he has participated in literary and performance festivals in Germany, India, and Japan. His poems have been translated into Dutch, English, German, Japanese, and Portuguese.

Stories and myths of Afrizal abound. He has been known to disappear for periods of time, to travel throughout Indonesia's villages and cities, and to write constantly, with his eyes and ears carefully attuned to the ever-shifting socio-political realities of the country. Afrizal claims that Indonesian is his first and only language. This assertion is particularly unusual for a poet from Indonesia, where most people have a "mother tongue" or "local language" as a first language; Indonesian, in which media and national discourse is conducted, as a second; and often either another local language or a foreign language, such as English, as a third.

During the *reformasi* period following the fall of Suharto's New Order regime in 1998, Afrizal quit writing and literary engagement for five years, working instead with Jakarta's Urban Poor Consortium (UPC) as an activist supporting anti-eviction and self-determination struggles in communities facing loss of livelihood and home in the name of development. After eventually leaving Jakarta and his work with the UPC, Afrizal lived for eight or so years in Solo and then Yogyakarta, a period of time in which he desired to become "nobody," maintaining a relative distance from literary and artistic community and living without books, endeavoring instead to write from his body and its immediate perceptions. It was during this period that Afrizal wrote, among other works, *Museum Penghancur Dokumen*. There are stories of Afrizal riding the Trans Jogja bus (Yogyakarta's public bus system) all day, from one end of the line to the other and back again, avoiding all conversation and writing in a little notepad.

While some elements of his literary persona may be apocryphal, the intensity and originality of Afrizal's writing is undoubtable. His poems are marked by repetition and variation, collage, parataxis, punning, dark humor, and alliteration. They often address Indonesia's colonial and postcolonial past and present through the objects and situations of day-to-day life in a perversely globalizing social climate, blurring the borders between embodied and semantic experience.

As I read through Afrizal's works available online and in bookstores, I found myself particularly drawn to *Museum Penghancur Dokumen*, perhaps because of its measured, contemplative feel. I began my translation with some poems from "Suara Yang Berjalan di Atas Kaca" ("Voices That Walk On Glass"), the final section of the book, struck by the astute language play that undermines the distinctions between reality and absurdity, constructing a robust, irreducible tonal space. For these first translations, I tried to enter that space and hang out awhile, familiarizing myself with its breath and temperatures, intuitively seeking English resonances.

Though this initial instinctual approach remained a guiding principle, going deeper into the work of the translations demanded a huge amount of contextualizing research and a constant questioning of the dynamic between authorial intent and readerly interpretation that's familiar to all acts of translation. The myriad complexities of translational decisions begin with the title: *Museum Penghancur Dokumen*. "Museum" and "dokumen" will of course be recognizable to English readers as cognates of the English "museum" and "document," absorbed into the polyglottal fibers of the Indonesian language. "Penghancur" is a noun corresponding roughly to the English "destroyer, crusher, smasher." However, following a logic of acute subversion that runs throughout the book, "museum penghancur dokumen" plays on "mesin penghancur dokumen"—roughly "document shredding machine" in English—or what is commonly called a "paper shredder" or "document shredder." So, if there were a way to embed a "museum" into the semantic space of the "machine" that could animate the act of "paper" or "document" shredding in the English language, that might be a more apt way of envisaging it.

These "machines," in both punning and more straightforward roles, pop up out throughout the book. "Mesin foto copy," "mesin cuci," "mesin hitung," "mesin pencetak," "mesin ATM," and "mesin penghancur dokumen" itself. Throughout, I've kept the literal "machine" in the English translation, even where unconventional, e.g. "printing machine" rather than "printer." Though this may be a rather facile illustration of the translational attitude of the book, I hope it suffices as an example of an intention to carefully follow Afrizal's poems in their attempt to lay bare the emptiness of rote linguistic commonplaces and fill their senselessness with possibilities for shadow meanings, unexpected imaginings.

In fact, the words "bayang," and "bayangan," which can be said to roughly mean both "shadow" and "imagination" (or, in the verb form "membayangkan," "to shadow" and "to imagine") appear with great frequency in *Museum Penghancur Dokumen*. Throughout the English version, I've translated the noun form as "shadow(s)" and the verb form as "to imagine." Though this decision is based in the context of the words' usage in the poems, in language situations where it's (almost universally) quite clear which meaning is being employed, I wonder if it's too consistent, too clean. Something about the indivisibility of ideas in this word, of shadow as imagination and imagining as shadowing, feels essential to the overall aesthetic and politic of the book.

And so, in the space of this note, I'd like to shadow an imagined version of this translation. Or, more accurately, a multitude of such possible versions. I think of *Document Shredding Museum* as a shadow of a shadow that will "slip away from its light." As Afrizal writes in the afterward, "The poems in this collection are like a piece of knitting that leaves its unknit leftover strands among the triangle's shadows: language-shadow, body-shadow, and space-shadow... leaving the dimensions unbound, reality discontinuous, memories unarchived in order to discover their own distinct skies." These poems invite us to discover for ourselves as well. They invite us to a "dinner party between *cause* and *effect*." Invite us to "swim in a language that always says *good morning* to the bathroom."

PART 1:
UNDER THE WORD RULER

ERASER'S GUEST

It's a shame this poem's already been erased when
I go to read it. Like humid air that tugs
at my arm to catch what will fall, is
falling, and falls. What's up with erasing? Glue,
scissors, and yarn make a shadow of barbed
wire. I erase the word *erase* from the documentation,
out from the barbed wire. Return every word
to glue, scissors, and yarn so as to
hide, lose, and erase once again
the word *erase*. And a knock
that's never been erased inside a shadow's
death: a guest from a door's shadow that's never
knocked on the door.

The guest suspects I don't have a chair to
die in, if I don't have a floor to live on. Waiting.
Waited on. Plans at 7pm. He serves the word
eraser from a bookstore to his guests,
like a shadow that'll slip away from its light.
You're my guest who I wait for from the mistake
of typing the word erase in a story about
a brilliant morning, and birds in flight
drifting away erasing their own chirps.

You don't have another chance to tidy what
can no longer be erased, after this poem. An eraser
causes 5 o'clock in the evening. Comes through til its
vacancy can no longer be seen.

USED LANGUAGE SHOPS A AND B

Junk shops A and B hang on to lots of
used languages A and B. Used dreams, used
sadness, used summers, all a little astonished
by languages A and B. A bit astonished slowly
beginning to walk a little and getting more astonished, and
beginning to run, becoming truly astonished, like other
explosions in the earlier silence: why do humans
make language between humans. Each day
they speak between humans in various
languages. Whatever they discuss between
humans, or whatever they narrate between
A and B. Whatever they finish of
whatever problem A or B. Either the problem is
their language, or their language is
the problem. A and B stare at each other: are
there humans who have never made language?
Mute from perception and used
document-cutting knives.

A used fan in junk shops A and B
can't stir the air into wind by
thinking. Powerless to provide coolness
to the conversation space. Used air, used
body, used humans. Make languages rub
against each other between the words *but, so, maybe,* and
if. A dinner gathering between *cause* and
effect. A parting of ways between *yes* and *no* in
a used blanket's fold. A broken fan and a
used fan. Neither knows if broken because used,
or used because broken. Or broken and used because
the rub of language dust.

My English language, language that gags the world,
gets more fluent listening to conversation,
translations pass by. Like A asks
B: "*B, are you well?*" When B goes to
answer A: "*A, I'm well,*" A's question has already
passed by, no longer A. Becoming a used question
for an answer that perfects the past.
B waits in front of the junk shop door. She
sees her age left behind in a used grammar
book. Lamentations of dry pages either
animal or human. My English language runs,
hunts, preys, gags my mother tongue
with used satellites.

All that's used is perfect. Perfect in
grammar that's passed by, is going on now,
and will come to pass in the by and by. A sees
B wearing A's used personality, which used to be seen as B. A
and B then turn on the electric dictionary. A little
slowly, then truly slowly, then collapse.

Their shadows fall, erasing used language
shops A and B into memories.

PHOTOGRAPHY GALLERY

How's it going? If I were to greet you with a dead camera that's freed itself from the first page of a photo book. *Great.* If you were to feel me inside you when you're outside yourself. A diagram of an angle of light composing darkness within its focus. *Click.* Releasing silent documentation, a body ill and left behind, scattered on the bookshelf, my diagram in vertical lines and your diagram in horizontal lines intersect me outside their frames. *Great.* The sound of horses' hooves among the archive's cadavers. Factory stink from above. *Click.* The air has hands when I collect strands of your hair from the white bedsheets. A sex act of humane death, in the middle of an epoch's funeral.

Click.
Great.
Could death take my picture.

SHARP PRISON

Beside me, a dictionary. To overthrow the body. To overthrow the clothes. Its pages poison in silence. Just a dictionary. Sharp. Bleeding. It'd been such a raucous, making barbed wire, either a bed or a grave. Just a dictionary. From the war of crafting a story. From the tale of crafting a god. Words fall into it, taking its edge. Taking its blood. Its eyes take its gaze. Make it so I can't see a long song about us. Groaning, like a photocopy machine in a shared mouth.

DRAGONFLY ABOVE A TALL FENCE

A paper on which I paint a field of stars, it's gray, the place where Tenzin Phuntsok self-immolated. Making grayer the gray of the paper. A paper on which I paint an estuary of fish fields, it's gray, the place where Chakgragunasegaran self-immolated. Making grayer the gray of the paper. The dictatorship of gray paper produces a putrid odor that plummets from the sky. As if there's carrion perpetually worshipped in the gray of the sky, a remembrance between a mung bean and a sunflower. Dragonflies flutter around, above a tall fence, immeasurable, between me and all me's. Make a morning from a dictionary emptied of names for time. Make a shrine over fact's death.

16th FLOOR MUSIC

I enter your body and now I'm outside your self. Do you still remember that heartbeat on a sofa? The red carpet that inhaled the floor. All that's yet to be ordered from your dreams dances with me. A dance about geese lost on the red carpet. Makes the difference between poetry and the whoosh of inhaled dirty air, between the blast of an embrace and a suitcase spending the night on the 16th floor of a hotel. I leave your body and now I'm inside your self. Do you still remember the tongue chained up in the mouth. Goofing around between the suitcase and poetry, between teeth and cut meat, an orgasm that stills the whole of human language. Somebody with black and white skin boils noodles in a kitchen that's going up to the 16th floor of a hotel. Keeps going up to build a different hotel, taller than your face ever gazing up into the dark. Me, I'm the lover who always empties his suitcase in your vagina.

TECHNIQUES TO ENTERTAIN THE VIEWER

The coffin's joy in saying happy new year.
I mean, *coffin* and *new year.*
Words move across it and fall like birds
shot in biology class.
Intellectuality that feels it could be a mediator
between body and reality, topples from the bookshelf.
I mean, *topples* and *bookshelf.*
Period and comma lost in a period and comma trap.
Words subjected to the dictionary's storm.
Split again between *storm* and *dictionary.*
A bossanova in the middle of a library fire.
Split again between *music* and *fire* in the library.
"Sir Entertainer," I say, so as to see my spirit
amongst a collection of housing costs and
football match tickets.
A wash bucket in a heap of city dwellers.
Applause of the perfume producers
and a printing press from a hospital.

Thank you.
Sir Viewer.
Thank you.

NAIL HOLES

I want to meet your body again. Because poems
are written on your shoulders. Like nail holes.
Untitled. I don't know who wrote them,
who planted nail holes inside.
It's written, *I will take myself.* It's written,
I dance in clothes that lose themselves.
And it's read too, *a singer vanished
inside silence's microphone.*

One sun becomes two suns. They
take turns glaring at me, between a hole and a nail,
between calling to me and driving me away. It's written again,
*about health and the smell of tobacco in the cracks of
your fingers.* I want to read it, *the procedure for freeing
death from a kiss.*
The smell of time from the nails' empty holes in your shoulders.
Holes covered over by other holes.

I'm still dragged around by my loose tooth, before
the nail is released from its hole. On your shoulders, it's written
*a lit-up body. A fire that puts out
its memories of silence and leaving.*

I scream to hear your voice. *It's written.*
I cry out to hear your footsteps, *it's written,*
falling all over and making a way to leave. On
your shoulders, love and silence never disagree
about poems that leave behind words. On
your shoulders ... a nail ... a soft-boiled egg ...

poems that poison language and recollection.

DECEMBER'S RULER

December is a straight ruler, very straight,
and broken in its straightness. A break
hidden in its fracture, a break that
looks out at stillness from its fracture.

And wind, and what groans below a ruler,
and speaking, and tomorrow — *January – January* – will
come along a past path. A path of scents
of spices, sugar, coffee, tobacco. Tobacco
that makes you cry all the way to the strait of Malacca.
Remember ships without rulers, remember the clop
of a horse carriage measuring your sorrow. About
December's statement, very straight and broken
in its straightness. And wind. Wind that
embroiders time from its rift.

Recall wind above a ruler and wind
below a ruler. And those that embroider
the rifts from break to break. A soul that changes
when time no longer follows movement: all
you've thrown remains in your hands. Break.
Recall above a ruler. All you've seen
remains in your eyes. Break. *Recall*
below a ruler. All you've said makes
your tongue like December bounding to
January. *Recall* pieces of December
that pick themselves up below a ruler
above a ruler. Break away from all
you've explained across from today.

December, December, a ruler that's stillness
within stillness.

That's straight and that's broken. That measures
all fractures. That looks out at January
like the ruler measuring your heartbeat.

That's not alone when it sees, when it sees a ruler
craft fields of stars across from today.

THERE'S NO MEANING: A REPEATING POEM

Workshop 1: Portrait Diagram

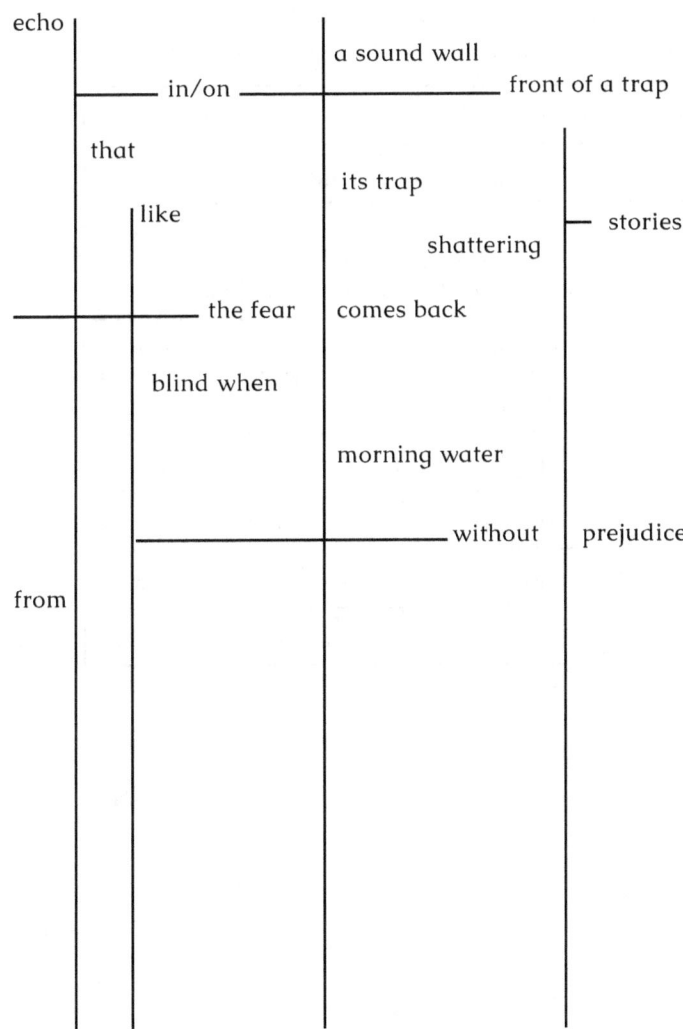

DOCUMENT SHREDDING MUSEUM

Workshop 2: Duration Editing

its voice's echo comes		back back back		to make		a sound wall	
of its voice	standing	in a circle	in	in	in	front of a globe	full of
time		traps	fingers that that that			clutch a rat	
and	and	and	its trap out out out			out back making din	
ner like		a shadow that that that that				leaves	of war
that are war			vomited	back	from from from		the fear of
its shape		shattering	laughing		stories stories store stories		of war
a mirror that goes			blind blinds blinds when it sees			the walls	
on the walls on the walls			withiiiiiiiin it and a sheet of hair				
on on-on on-on on		the morning	paper water that		crosses thethethethethe		
bridge		over	the river over its droplets without without				
without		prejudice in the face			of dry dry dry dry leaves		
that	keep echoes						

of
the
forest

AFRIZAL MALNA

Workshop 3: To See

its voice's echo comes back to make a sound wall of its voice standing in a circle in front of a globe full of time traps fingers that clutch a rat and its

trap out back making dinner like a shadow that leaves its shape shattering laughing war stories vomited back from the fear of

a mirror that goes blind when it sees the walls within it and a sheet of hair on the morning paper water that crosses the bridge over the river

over its droplets without prejudice in the face of dry leaves that keep echoes of the forest

Workshop 4: To Look

its
voice's
echo
comes
back
to
make
a
sound
wall
of
its
voice
standing
in
a
circle
in
front
of
a
globe
full
of
time
traps
fingers
that
clutch
a
rat
and
its
trap
out
back
making
dinner
like
a
shadow
that

leaves
its
shape
shattering
laughing
war
stories
vomited
back
from
the
fear
of
a
mirror
that
goes
blind
when
it
sees
the
walls
within
it
and
a
sheet
of
hair
on
the
morning
paper

water
that
crosses
the
bridge
over
the
river
over
its
droplets
without
prejudice
in
the
face
of
dry
leaves
that
keep
echoes
of
the
forest

Workshop 5: My Captive

its voice's echo comes back to make a sound wall
of its voice
standing in a circle
in front of a globe full of time traps
fngers that clutch a rat
and its trap out back making dinner
like a shadow that leaves its shape
shattering, laughing, war stories
vomited back from the fear of
a mirror that goes blind when it sees
the walls within it
and a sheet of hair on the morning paper
water that crosses the bridge
over the river
over its droplets
without prejudice in the face of dry leaves
that keep echoes of
the forest

PART 2:
ARCHIVE SHADOWS

POETRY SEMINAR AT THE SUNDA STRAIT
  for Goenawan Mohamad

A night table made of wood, cigarette butts
stubbed out on its surface. We eat together.
Vague night in the middle of the city. A
revolution switches feet, aboard a battleship
parked in the Sunda Strait. A
treaty to pick oneself up: right feet
amputated – left feet amputated. Don't know
whether to walk or to not walk. Don't know whether
to sit or to stand. The smell of sulphur from the slopes
of Krakatau repaints the maps above
bleating words.

An independence not devised by
screaming: the enemy is outside the gate, but
inside the gate too. A republic imagined
in the back door. A man in the glass
door: doesn't know whether he's going out or
coming in. Back and forth walk the sleep-deprived
Indonesian researchers, in an exhausted
Indonesian language. A bank amidst armies of
peace. I'm with you, in an old
car, a man like that jackfruit tree, we stare
at each other but don't see each other. A book of poetry
in a woman's lap.

"Where are we? Looking at words, as if a mother's
death."

A door, who knows if it's at the back of the house or
the front of the house. A glass door through which
to look out through which to look in. A word to
silence the slogans. A Sukarnoist who keeps

a postcard of the Statue of Liberty in his coat
pocket. A hoarse love song by Leonard
Cohen: *Dance Me to the End of Love.*
Cigarette smoke of the leader's training,
between a train and the storm of a party. A
man holds back his tears in the corner
of a restaurant. "I stepped out of a local newspaper,
as a teenager, in a small village, amidst the revolutions
of 3 cities. And a novel about the crimes of the guerrilla
armies, on pages equipped with alarms."

A show poster. Does the show go on
outside or inside? How could Kunti
send her child drifting away? Karna, how,
Karna? How could the sun create you
from arrows, and pick you back up again
on a red morning? How could Caligula
sink common sense into a nation's
finances? Tell the story once again, Caesonia, how
I entrusted love to your embrace, when
all went mad in the hands of your husband. The powers
that be have taken the moonlight from the fields
of our thoughts. How could poetry enable us to walk
with our own shadow, through our selves
still asleep on a train?

A ticket-taker and a guy who
sells water in a magazine office. A
journalist who aims with words. A
camera at the base of language. And a man
in the glass window. A magazine offce, its
construction rooted in the 19th century, before the world
war, before trading spices for a
nation. A sugar road that built the railway
from Klaten to Amsterdam. That man, his shadow
outside and his shadow inside. The scent of tobacco

alters the memory of the coat he'd worn,
either the color of dirt or even darker
than sand. A color that repaints history
the same color. A scent of tobacco that clasps
sadness in a ventilation hole.

"Have I been traitorous to you, mother, so that
you won't give birth again to a killer?"

The air-conditioned 2 in the morning air reminds him of
a jungle of words. A republic on the second
floor, right? And a fght over where to put
the stairs to the second foor, between rainy
season and the sugar plantations we've burnt.
A revolution between feet that switch position.
A night that I tuck into a book of the history
of modern Indonesian poetry. *A cold impossible to record* on
the page. And *remnants of moonlight* before
the eclipse. Equipped with a thousand slogans to
clasp the sadness puddling on the second
foor. The morning sunlight survives above.
For hope, for the old ladies selling rice
at the public market. Is it. Is historical materialism
dead, in a psychology course about
social class? Is it. Is revolution
erased, inside a merchant ship sailing
along a path of fire? Forming phantom militias to
overthrow our common vitality. Is it. About.
But.

The man stands at the top of the stairs and goes down to
the first floor. It's like he's walking on the stairs forever. Each
time he takes a step, it's like the stairs keep growing
almost faster than his steps themselves.
It's his steps that form the stairs
rather than the stairs themselves.

Is he going down – is he going up.
Putting time into a train with
each of his steps. Giving me a word to
not say anything at all about the wound that
grows on the first page of national history.
And about my own self that still smells
the thought of a hat you've worn. A thought
that tries to change a sob into
light rain, a vague afternoon among leaves
that grow voluminously. Freedom is nursed
in a gamble between Duryudana and
Yudhistira.

I recognize that man. Someone who walks
with a voice like kneaded newsprint.
A voice between poetry and word rubble. He's like
a morning amidst the vague crowds of
night. He wants to take up the revolution
again, with an opera about silence.

"We've seen a mother make a
scar on a tiger's mouth." For friends
and a word that can't be said: a wind
that ships salt, minds the rainy season
in the North. In here.

NOT ABOUT BEING BROKEN
(a bridge from Murtidjono)

He brings a ladder for the bridge below.
About the passage down and then up.
Crosses through a suitcase about what's above. A bridge
and a bridge between a plant and a plant,
about coming down and budding. Letting out
Javanese oxygens, moving across a poem by fingers
afraid of grammar. Brings a ladder for wind and
theater, and politics in humid lungs.
He brings a ladder to drop in on bile,
white blood beneath a papaya leaf. He crosses over
comes down and walks on. An empty suitcase
emptied, gendhing moving across
contemporary art and a smoke shop. He brings
a ladder to warm the roots of silence.
Walks with Gendon and Halim playing
Gatoloco, a bridge for Bedoyo and Martha
Graham. A broken ladder from philosophies of
chicken and spinach.

He brings the breaks together again, because there are
friends, because yesterday is in this morning. There's always
yesterday for a broken ladder. There's always
today for coming down and moving across. A ladder that
comes down to its breaks and breaks. Comes down to plant
music in love's notation. A ladder with
Sadra, moving across the secrets of sounds that don't make a noise.
He brings a ladder across the break between electrical
currents and a theater-goer. A room for
the mystery of the crosser. A ladder about
moving across with Prapto and Gundono, about
a fire under the Solo River. Keeps each
Javanese letter for those that sing below

about not being above. A ladder for those who
wake in the noontime, erasing morning
from the smell of coffee and stories under a pillow.

What bridge is a man? What ladder is a
death, my friend? We didn't have time to hug,
to make a bridge on which to not be afraid of not
having a ladder. To swallow laughter to our backbone,
to smile under an electric guitar. To oil our hair so
time like art crosses through the years. A ladder
that moves across broken moving across coming down.
Send Solo, the city, on an airplane flying about
dance and medicated oil, book ladders and cigarette smoke.

He says no, not about being afraid not
about being broken.

DOCUMENT SHREDDING MACHINE

Let's go, drink up. No. I'm not being es kelapa
muda. Eat up in that case, *please.* No. I'm
not being nasi rames. Come in to my bathroom,
please if you're not thirsty, if you're not hungry,
if you're bored of eating. Allow me to bestow
friendliness on you, for all the longing that
destroys the walls of my ego. How can
I go out if you don't come in.

You can hear my bathroom bathing
grammar, in the tempter's hands of a TV poet.
Allow me to lead you by your hand. Come
in here which is over there. Nowadays which are bygone days.
Come in if you don't like grammar. *Please*
if it's like that, exchange your clothes with my clothes.
The washing machine washed them after I got drunk, after
I cried, after I killed myself 12 minutes
ago. Imagine my body in those empty clothes.
Please read your sorrows:

"Yesterday I was bored, today I'm bored, tomorrow
yesterday's boredom will come again." What, does grammar
have to change into an ice cream museum so that
you're not bored? *Please.* Everything that's done in
the name of language, it's a mask of fire. Market
that replaces your body with a document shredding
machine. *Please,* I'm only a somebody in
proses like this, a tourist erupting
inside a dictionary. A sulky poem
in the corpse craw of a poet.
Please, put me to sleep in your untranslated
silence. Document shredding machine
alone in your sagas.

BETEL CHALK BLAST PROCESS

The chunk of betel chalk starts by being soaked in water. The water
starts distributing hot air. The coral-like forms start emitting
smoke into the puddle of water and the puddle of steam
above it. Like a word leaving its form
in a fire. Chalk inside a betel leaf
that burns the floor of your tongue. The shapes start
falling off like hills that melt and explode in bursts.
The surface of the chalk will appear
transformed into white mud, its tenderness hot. The chalk will
appear between blackboards. Chalk mud in
smoking bubbles, boiling noise, and its
blasts hold hot steam up to
the tip of the tongue. The shards of bubbles
smoke. The chalk erases a history lesson
from the blackboard, after the school bell
sounds. As if something will erupt inside
the chalk mud, metaphors that make
hot steam turn into a blackboard. Evicting black shadows from
their black and from their blasts. This process will
stop when history takes a holiday, and the whole
chunk of chalk changes into thick white chalk
mud. The steam stares at shards of
bubbles. My hands and feet clutch at
bursts of steam. And the tongue ... where's the tongue in
the black shadows of steam? The chalk is hot. The
blackboard is chalk dust flying off in all directions.
Fingers will blister. The sharp pain of
peeling skin emits the dead lice
inside it. The chalk falls.
Walls will be white inside
the chalk. A process that tempts me to
pick up my bedroom and put it in
a smoking letter-sized envelope. A task that feels

useless, but I observe the explosion process
when releasing the pressure of hot air, and the envelope
blasts silence open: a poem's mouth vomits
talk of leaving. A bedroom that
stores shadows of embraces and sucked
betel chalk blasts.

A bottle of door shadows. A bottle of betel chalk.
Both paint my dreams into pre-dreaming.

SPICE BRIDGE

Agarwood ❈ Anise ❈ Basil ❈ Bay leaf ❈ Black pepper ❈ Black temu ❈ Candlenut ❈ Caraway ❈ Cardamom ❈ Cassumunar ginger ❈ Chili pepper ❈ Cinnamon bark ❈ Clove ❈ Copal ❈ Coriander ❈ Dammar gum ❈ Daughter temu ❈ Bridge from kitchen seasonings to the blood of Columbus ❈ Eucalyptus bark ❈ Fragrant pandan ❈ Frankincense ❈ Gambier ❈ Garlic ❈ Ginger ❈ Greater galangal ❈ Indigo ❈ Joke temu ❈ Kaffir lime ❈ Key lime ❈ Key temu ❈ Laurel ❈ Lemon pepper fruit ❈ Lemongrass ❈ Mace ❈ Massoy bark ❈ Mango temu ❈ Mustard ❈ Nutmeg ❈ Onion ❈ Bridge from perfume to the blood of Vasco da Gama Tabasco ❈ Peppercorn ❈ Red ginger lily ❈ Rose ❈ Safflower ❈ Sand ginger ❈ Sandalwood ❈ Sappanwood ❈ Scallion ❈ Screwpine leaf ❈ Shallot ❈ Shampoo ginger ❈ Sour mangosteen ❈ Suji ❈ Sweet lime ❈ Tamarind ❈ Temu giring ❈ Temu rapet ❈ Turmeric ❈ Vetiver ❈ White temu ❈ Ylang-ylang ❈ Bridge from medicines to a fortress of ladies wreathed in red roses ❈ Anise ❈ Cassumunar ginger ❈ Chili pepper ❈ Clove ❈ Dammar gum ❈ Ginger ❈ Lemon pepper fruit ❈ Mace ❈ Sandalwood ❈ Sesame seed ❈ Sour mangosteen ❈ Tamarind ❈ Temu tis ❈ Vanilla ❈ Vetiver ❈ Bridge from Diogo Lopes de Mesquita to the blood of Ternate ❈ Agarwood ❈ Black pepper ❈ Candlenut ❈ Caraway ❈ Cardamom ❈ Cinnamon bark * Coriander ❈ Eucalyptus bark ❈ Frankincense ❈ Gambier ❈ Ginger ❈ Key lime ❈ Safflower ❈ Sand ginger ❈ Turmeric ❈ Ylang-ylang ❈ Bridge of fire forever sending ships to your archives

FIRE IN A BRIEFCASE

"A cold beer," between two separate sentences, and
"a cold beer," between two shooting targets.

I'm a politician. He always carries
his briefcase from office to office. Cities, confict statistics, and
blood thinners. He sees the public as pulsing
earth, a trickle at the neck, protein threat nearing sleep.
I'm a politician, I mean, without the slightest doubt. Calculations
of divisions of opinion either within or without my briefcase.

He closes his briefcase, like a bullet separating
two sentences.

"A cold beer," he says, between those two separate sentences. I don't want a condom or a beard trimmer in my briefcase. Once again in my briefcase, a speech ratifying a measure against making a state outside the state. Thumbs up brand. Against debasing humanity in a house of prayer, between two separate sentences looking at a needle and a pair of scissors
on the dining table.

A bullet, he says, like intelligence lost
among political theories and a bottle opener.
Sound of gunshots barraging words. A pillow swallows the bed.
A briefcase burns all it holds.

He runs to save his briefcase, that politician,
with the fire still ablaze inside.

FOR SIR LIFE

I boil rice to feed my dogs. It reminds me sometimes of hungry moments—"good evening gentlemen gut worms"—I pick up each grain of spilled rice. Gather them one by one to build a fortress on the tip of my tongue. Postpone all the feelings around human life. A hungry ceremony on the list of fears and sympathies.

My dogs,
rice grains,
me,
a fortress,

all gathered together.
Circling round a hungry stove.

A POLICY PROPOSAL FOR THE POLICE

> "Gentlemen, I can guarantee you that our governance is no longer popular, either with the peasants or with the native officials, large and small ... A feeling of dissatisfaction is spreading, both among the noblemen and the commoners, regarding the way the government is managed and justice upheld. Since the end of 1900, a kind of terrorist movement has appeared ... or even a resistance movement against the government. It seems the central government bureaucracy doesn't understand the meaning of all of this." (P.J.F. Van Heutsz, 1904—1906)

I'm inflicted with my own arrival there and here. Looking
at the failure that, to be honest, is in everything I make. Amidst
machines and systems in a hole of silence, buying and
selling throw each other away. Entertainment and things
bought here and there. Memories in the rubble
of change. Leftover debt in an unlocked casket. Rainy season
speeches in every drowned channel of justice. Dirt
and the crackling of fire on the dinner table. You and I stand here.
But we never stand together.

I photograph the palm of my hand, as if photographing an
archipelago made of paper pulp. Perpetual expenditure
there and here, longer than the road I walk forward
and back. The sound of rice grains scraping against a pan
like economic data that's lost its adding machine. My heart
drowns in history's games and clothes fit for going to heaven.
Financial statements that stroll along the year's end. Vitality
that turns to rubble in the commerce of data science,
there and here. Health prophesied by vitamin C
and a toothbrush. I'm inflicted with my own arrival,
buying silence, clean air, and the job
market.

Gentlemen, can failure be photographed, so we can see
how we laugh and smile.
Can we photograph a toothbrush in the middle of vitality's
ruins chronically raped and pillaged from there and
from here. Vitality that becomes a toy for the use
capacity of violence. Population growth reports
that turn to fire at dinnertime.

Gentlemen, can we read anew, from
the pointless alphabet. And they fashion
a language from each failure, from each wound's history
there and here, from a Saturday night farewell
dance. Here we stand, like plants
waiting for a gardener. Not letting an
archipelago become a collective sewage ditch.

Gentlemen. There and here. The rainy season's
gone blue in your city.

ACTIVITIES OF ICE BLOCKS

The kids know their bodies are unnumbered
blocks of ice. They melt to
fall in love. They melt to get a job.
They melt to buy shoes. And turn
back into ice blocks. They melt to be
ice blocks. They become ice blocks to melt.
They become ice blocks to go home.
Become ice blocks to go to school. They freeze
and melt like water kept in
an ice box.

At 6 in the morning they start melting in order to become ice blocks
around 1 in the afternoon. They want to make
a sun in the middle of the night. A sun below political
weather. A night roof that tosses history like
electricity that's gone out. Don't think you're a hero just because
you hurt others. A country like a stomach full of
stones. At 8 in the evening the ice blocks flow, seeking the
lowest temperatures, so they can freeze. Little by little, their brains and
hearts start turning to ice. Kidneys. Bile.
Ice blocks.

Ice blocks give off cold air. Ice blocks. So
cold, ice blocks. A cold that cripples the current
of ice blocks' electricity. A cold that makes you ignorant:
Am I, am I inside or outside of that
cold air? Am I a panicked ice block? Am
I a stone quarreling with stories
in the middle of freezing?

Time beats so cold in your city.

AFRIZAL MALNA

ROCK IN A SHOE

Good morning Kamsudi, *good morning* Busro, *good morning* Remy and angry Aidil. We're still here,
at yesterday's oxtail soup warung, yesterday's cup of coffee,
yesterday's ashtray and plastic chair. We're still tending to
a rock that we've kept in our shoes.
We take a picture of our bodies in front of the coffee
shop, next to the dumpster. White hair falls
from our heads after holding back laughter,
and yesterday's still here.

Good morning, time. Good morning all that's
replaced our night with little
stories. Time that wears away our bedroom
ceiling, before we have the chance to sleep soundly, peeking in
at dreams through moldy walls. Almost 50
years we've waited for our shoes to come back
changed into leather. Time, like
uncanny beings whose offspring inhabit
our bodies. Poetry that even now doesn't know
how to write it: 12 blankets for
my friends from Makassar, 12 blankets for
my friends from Padang and Lampung.

And tomorrow, tomorrow we'll come back to yesterday's
warung, to yesterday's Jalan Cikini that's
rendered our bodies as time's attempt
at waiting, waiting's attempt at being capable
of seeing, seeing's attempt to recognize
your unexpected arrival. The governors in this city
come and go, like playthings in
colonial cities. Make egg cartons for poetry
and theater. Yesterday. We — we never know
about today and tomorrow. And the rock is ever

deeper, ever harder, between the shoe and the leather.
A rock — for all the nations too suspicious of
freedom, of poverty, and the people who
keep on walking with their feet.

DON'T FORGET THE SHALLOTS

The electricity was dead. That morning. I don't need electricity
to plant rice in the fields. That morning. I was sure
that birds made my ears, together with the wind
coming in from the south. The wind dramatized
my ears so they'd listen in to insects and jackfruit
sap, like an 18th century opera in the folds
of my hat. I planted rice, liquid earth beneath
the soles of my feet, soft fields where stars
leave night. And seeds that loyally
look after this planet.

Hey Pak Kerto, Mbah Surip, hey Mbah Harjo, Bu Kerto,
cow's moos and jackfruit have made the fragrant
earth and insects in a hat's folds. Water from
Merapi has carried in black stones, scraps of
the gods' bodies after the war. That morning.
Hey, water and the smell of sulphur, tempeh and
tofu cadavers in the river. Cadavers from the parties
of city people who eat from 500,000 rupiah plates.

Hold this, feel it, how morning makes
your throat orange. Time doesn't choose a religion
to differentiate your body from the birds.
Hold it, what are you working on right now? Hold
it, can't you see for yourself what I'm doing right
now? Hold it, are you sure of what you're
doing right now? I've clutched it tight, deeper
and deeper into my palms. Are you unsure
of what I'm doing right now? So deep
into my palms that there I am between
silence and emptiness. The electricity was dead. That morning.

Batik clothing, batik cloth, leaves to feed
the goats. Are you sure the electricity was dead, that morning?
I'm sorry, are you sure of what you're working on?
It's like there's a dry season in my hands. That's why I'm
asking you. That morning. Ask, what are you doing
right now? Hey batik clothing. Hey. Electricity. Dead.
See for yourself, am I planting rice right now? Not
an electric carcass.

If there weren't hotels suddenly standing on
our fields, if there weren't airplanes hauling
goods from the city, hold our hands and
the rainy season comes with gray plastic ponchos,
we'll harvest 100 days from now, 2 km's distance from
here. You'll taste the scent of red rice. Red
rice that doesn't require the chitchat of politics
in order to be poor. Clutch my hand tight, where
the sun plants vitamin C. There's no one
in my hands, except for reddened vitamin C.

Oh, Lento screens the Battle of Surabaya film,
Tuan Malaby shot at close range.
The provocateur who seized the RRI radio mic. Don't bring
that history to our rice fields. Careful, the electricity's
dead. Oh, Radhar tells of the evils committed
in the Ramayana. Making Hanuman into
a white monkey on account of the betrayal he faced
in Sri Lanka. Southern nations
leaving ships and their seas in history's
storms. Why does his excellency doubt my honorable
behavior? Mataram of yore left the palace,
that morning.

Hey, *Your Excellency of That Morning*, don't uproot my rice plants, don't
read my rice like you're reading the paper. This isn't
that morning's printing, this isn't that morning's paper. 2 km

before lunch. 21,000 feet above
sea level, from Yogyakarta to Surabaya. Hey
Ram, Mei, Sari, funny, huh, how rice plants can be read
like the paper? Have the fields already turned
into the paper? Maybe in a minute our fields will
turn into a TV, right. Funny, ya know. That morning. I see electricity
saunter around the city, bathing in morning sunlight.
We'll eat the newspaper after the harvest, right, the harvest
of scrap paper politics.

That morning. That morning. You always make us
unsure of what we're doing.

WINTER SEMINAR

His stomach's made of fried noodles. It's not cold out tonight, he says. Then he puts on a jacket. I'm waiting for you to die, and I'd like to sleep with you, he says. His hands are made of plastic straws. I don't have any plans tonight, he says. Just want to sleep and forget all my work. Then he puts on a jacket. His stomach's made of palm oil, and night air caught in his large intestine. My girlfriend doesn't know that I'm a poet, he says, putting on a jacket. But poetry drives me to hate language teachers, as he puts on a jacket. As he puts on a jacket, my stomach's made of fried noodles and it's not too cold out tonight. It's not too cold out, I tell him, and don't wear a jacket to find out just how hungry I am tonight. 4 hours from Denpasar, drowning myself in sleep. At a coffee shop, young prostitutes on Braga. A photo of Mick Jagger, huge, hung up at the intersection. A train station from Holland. Sitor's seminar at Erasmus Huis, Rendra's seminar in *Pikiran Rakyat*. Wianta's book is still being edited. I never think about culture inside your jacket, he says. Look, all this is just raw material. Nothing's happened yet. Nothing's meant yet. The cold is only in your jacket.

CHINESE ID CARD
    for Lan Zhenghui

I've prepared a backpack, beard trimmer
and a nationality photographed at
the district offce. Every time I fly, I'm afraid
I'll miss the plane. Or find myself
falling in love with Mandarin in someone else's room.
Last Tuesday hasn't arrived. Tomorrow's still tomorrow.
Who knows where yesterday will go before Sunday. Tuesday
is still waiting for the yesterday that hasn't arrived.
Tuesday isn't Tuesday if it isn't yet Tuesday.

Tomorrow, Tuesday will start hollowing out my fantasies,
to hear Mandarin from my narrow eyes.
Tomorrow's still tomorrow before yesterday. Tuesday
doesn't keep 100 years of each generation's
fear of state ID cards and the job
market. People make a house to
tell their lies in. Scream a generation scattered on
an escalator's steps. And scream again their
fears atop the Great Wall.

Are you from Indonesia? the taxi driver asks. *Yeah,*
I answer. Like answering the cries of the shops
razed in Jakarta. The women
stripped naked and raped. Bodies
turned into burnt charcoal. History that
grabs our hands and plunges
them over and over again into the same wound. The wound
that comes back asking: *are you from Indonesia?*

That morning the electrical wires along the street still held back
the cold, shaking off remnants of night, grease, and
Olympic fireworks. A friend ordered a

Mao hat. What I remember about this country
from the Great Wall, weasel fur hats from Mongolia,
political reproofs from Tibet, waterfalls of humanity
spilling from a hole in the sky — to the communist
management that regulates the residents' income
all the way up to my hotel room.

Zhenghui, I admire your paintings, that return
to rice paper pulp and Chinese ink. The wind
approaching winter starts to greet your neck.

NEW ORDER ARCHITECTURE IN YOUR HOME

I'm in your kid's room. 2.5 x 2.5 meters. A fan
and a painting that's not really my taste.
Who knows why, I feel like an idiot faced with
that painting. At dawn, you'd already left for
dialysis. The whole hospital became a bathtub
for you to wash your blood in. The painting, the blood, and
the hospital make me feel alone here.
I walk to the bathroom, like walking without
kidneys, and one step more — without my self. On top
of the pillows you laid out a yellow button-down shirt, a white
t-shirt size L, for me to change into. I don't know:
how can I wear that size L t-shirt
without my self. That yellow button-down, these days it's in
my dresser in Nitiprayan.

I've already eaten the breakfast your maid cooked.
But I didn't eat the fish, it tasted like eating
everything that stinks inside my body. Housing complexes
dried out from New Order architecture, here. The kind
that hack space into pieces like a lighter with
gasoline beside it. I'm with the octopus of electric
cables at the crossroads of your home. Braids of water
pipes jumble into the gutter. From that
gutter your maid cleans the door mat, like
cleaning the filth you brought home from
a trip. A tailor passes by the house, time after
time, on a pitiful bicycle.

A little pond in front of your house, its fish
like animate plastic. And a different tailor
comes back, passing by with the same poignancy.
Here, I'm like that tailor, even more a kidney,
strangled by architecture that hates humanity.

That trades leaves for glass and iron. That
replaces wind with a twirling propeller. In
each house, the butts of air-conditioners, like boils
growing on the windows, squirt their hot air
into my kidneys. The stories of your politics, ever
more inflamed, and all the roads as if made out of
lighters.

Friend, I'm already in the taxi, and heading for
a different hospital. Dropping in on the heart of a
nation, amidst the tailors who don't know anymore what
needs to be tailored.

UNDER GATOLOCO'S GAMELAN

I met Gatoloco in a flashlight. He
shined his flashlight eyes day and night.
His body just an unblemished shadow spanning day
and night, on Jalan Selamet Riyadi day and night in Solo
I met him. *Why are you still here, like this?* I asked
and I heard the moan of an old banyan's
language, elephant feet, bulletless Bedoyo dance
pistol in each of his unblemished shadow's holes.

The Solo intercity bus terminal late at night and late
night. The little people lug their children
their belongings in cardboard boxes crumpled bags clove cigarette
smoke. A solo organ player exits
the bus bound for Jakarta old and crumpled. Sips a coffee
at the terminal warung, inviting the remnants of his fatigue
to drink with him. A flashlight shone out
of his eyes too: *I don't know where to go or
that life would turn out like this.* Gatoloco's unblemished shadow
blankets my throat and shoulders, dragging along a salty
dry season. *You want an
oldy?* the organ player asks. *I can
sing all the old ones,* he says.
*I used to entertain the folks on a ship that
searched for love on the seas and southern storms,* he says.

Buses come and go from different cities, people
come and go bringing night from different cities.
The city comes and goes through the bus door. Bus
wheels jacket bag becak scooter taxi — majestic
whores. The toilet's a thousand rupiah ... Semarang ... Purwokerto
... Surabaya ... Cirebon ... oh Tuban ... Bandung...
Tegal ... Cikampek ... Gatoloco began to play
the gamelan inside the shadow. You could hear the shadow's sounds

build another terminal. The people as if
seeing the air were the gendhing that he played. *Why
does it feel like I'm hearing the sound of a shadow, here, like
this?* Then they saw the buses coming and going begin to turn
into shadows of buses coming and going, their feet began to turn
into shadows of their feet, their children and spouses
began to turn into shadows of their children and spouses.
The whole terminal became an unblemished shadow throughout
the night.

Gatoloco invited me out as if dragging away
language's groan. Train sounds, falling rocks,
shrieking sand, oh wounded gamelan. I watched
my body sinking deeper, a night that goes,
taking his flashlight which plants itself
in every played gendhing.

CRYPTIC NEWS FROM DARMO GANDUL

He said 100 years, I've wanted to be a good person he
said. And I keep my tongue in a branch of the kapok tree
in my backyard I said. He said
100 years, I've wanted to be a lovely person he said. And
I keep my eyes in a neon lamp in my backyard I said. He said 100 years,
I've wanted to be a person who says *welcome* to
everything that comes he said. And I keep my feet
in a stone where ghosts reminisce about humanity.

I've wanted to be a person who says *I wish you health and happiness*
to everyone I meet he said 100 years. And
I keep my hands in a river where the fish and
the sand reminisce about humanity. Nowadays my body, without eyes tongue feet
hands, I keep in the rain in my backyard.
I whisper to my kidneys and lungs I whisper to
my heart and intestines I whisper ... *you're the rain of a dusk
that's yet to be created.*

Now you bring that dusk an ear of clearest
silence. An ear made from demolished homes
from soil that stiffens the wind that can no longer blow.
Leaves make a tree from the clouds. I place cryptic news
inside it in order to forget myself. And tomorrow — *let's go* —I've
become the one who forgets language.

SEMINAR ON LUNTO KLOOF

Iron from coal. Cement factories from coal. Houses from coal. Trains from coal. Underground hollows from coal. Prisons from coal. Hospitals from coal. Laborers from coal. History from coal. Cars from coal. Language from coal. Bay harbors from coal. Wives from coal. Markets from coal. Keroncong from coal. Swimming pools from coal. Sate Madura from coal. Death from coal. Mohamad Yamin from coal. Tan Malaka from coal. Sujatmoko from coal. Lovers from coal. WH van Greve from coal. The year 1892 from coal. New year's parties from coal. The Ombilin River from coal. Hugs from coal. Salt from coal. Corruption from coal. Hills sawed apart from coal. Hilltops fallen from coal. Drains drifting away from coal. Jungles collapsed from coal. Tomorrow ... I've been atop it all, 21,000 feet above the morning radio broadcast.

LAST STATION STOP
for Slamet Gundono

I'm only a pretty lie sprawled out on the 230-kg floor of
my name. A name half made of tears
and the dawn call to prayer. A pretty lie that can laugh
and sing from my life itself. A pretty lie from
coastal lyrics that give me the ability
to laugh with God. To look at heaven from those
who ask, *why is there an echo of silence
when I stand and reach out towards all that's blind
around me? Why is my asking like not saying
anything at all?*

For 30 days I forgot how to sleep. The walls
started to talk, reversed the gravity between
my body and the night that's left at 11 in the morning.
All the world came skirmishing into
my ear. I pulled the breaks on the train, screeching, the
smooth gliding iron suddenly stopping, screeching, as if
the enormous iron came crashing into its last station stop.
I spewed up my body along with voices anxious
to encounter the names of their longing.

I live with Bisma who walks with
1,000 arrows in his back, loyalty and blind honesty
23,000 feet above sea level. Solitude
beat the 230-kg of my body to a pulp. Javanese palace
made of gamelan, a woman dances with
milk spilling steadily from her breasts:
I'm there between the stones that *will* shatter
and *have yet* to shatter.

My palms are full of my own saliva.
A bowl of tea for the sintren lost in

my lyrics. I see my body in the TV like
a nation raped by its own masses. The gravitational
pull of the TV that makes my body become 2
meters long, *shit*, I pissed my pants.

At that last station stop, I draw my own
lungs, soil steadily sloughing off without end
sloughing off soil sloughing off. Until I smell
the rain from wayang puppets that play themselves
between the stones that *will* shatter and *have yet* to shatter
between the lyrics that *will* cast spells and *have yet* to cast spells
between the keris that fall out from my silence and
have yet to fall out.

RAINCOAT IN TWO CITIES

That city became Semarang since the seawater wanted
to climb the hill and have a new year's party in the space inside
colonial buildings. Drink friendship
and paint your photo on the rainy season's walls.
All night long it wears an electrical raincoat:
the city floating 45 degrees above history.
In its raincoat, clove cigarettes and an ATM card.
College students cluster in a coffee shop, taking
literature, communications, anthropology, and
study hours from glass shards. I'm the kid
that can play electric bass, blues
with riot scraps and a busted comb. I've
flooded the job market and civil servants'
wage raises. The architects that design
the city with seawater and rain.

Let me reach the brink, for the traces that
make their own openings.

A train comes out the mouth of the Yogyakarta station, smelling
of tobacco from art parties and fried beef. I
breathe again after the thousands of city billboards
are my eyes that spin on and on, aching
time. The train rails hang on to their Dutch East
India Company shares until Semarang. Palace grounds that
hang on to chicken eggs, a blue raincoat still
singing Portugese keroncong. Scent of sugar cane, scent of rice fields,
red brinks burnt. I'm in Yogyakarta by now
after successfully becoming someone who's too busy to shower for 2
days, using excel for my tight
schedule. And a cold beer between appointments.
I've come to two cities over a two-hour trip
continued by bike at 6 in the morning. Let me reach

the brink, for the traces that make
their own openings. A city made of 6
in the morning, and I trust in it like a bell that
rings without ringing, the shadow of a mountain before
blue and before gray and before here.

CLAPPING BEHIND A FENCE
  for Cahyo, the guitarist who always plays from his tears

It is forgotten. Picked up again. Done again. In 50
more steps, pick up a new pebble. The pebble from 50
steps ago is put down. Like standing. Resembling
squatting. Walk another 50 steps
looking out for a new pebble. Replace the pebble from
50 steps ago. Someone claps their hands behind
a fence. Like walking. Almost squatting. Choosing
a pebble. And 50 steps not walked again. Like
a ceremony. My body is like a ceremony of baffing
silence.

Every 50 steps one pebble is put down and another
pebble picked up. A crowd, alone and
clapping. It's not the fence that claps
its hands. A crowd, alone and clapping
behind the fence. As if remembering the long ago.
Memorizing how people learn to walk,
to squat, 50 steps and pick up another pebble
and put down another pebble. Feel the new with
the old. Feel again the movement and the step,
forgetting what must be asked and answered.
Forgetting in order to remember what's not frozen.
Solitude claps its hands in the middle of a crowded
fence.

People live clapping their hands behind a fence. A pebble
comes from each decaying clap — from
the decay of hand claps. The crowd doesn't
see there's someone crying behind the fence. The lone
someone sees that fellowship has been felled behind
the fence. The crowd drives motorbikes. Doesn't know
about 50 steps and about the pebbles and about

the lone someone weeping behind the fence. And this
is about how the pebbles exchange themselves for one another. Not
building a fence and not building hand claps.

About someone walking 50 steps forward 50
steps backward 50 steps to the side 50
steps inwards. Ever more inwards than forward and
backward. Song of a me that's
here.

MERAPI DINNER

Merapi vomits Jakarta. This is green lava. This
is brown lava. Straight, like a ruler measuring
your calf. Please, choose to be photographed. Please, take a photo.
Please, take a photo. Gentlemen, there's a hot cloud in the way
You drive your cars. Looking
for a hand-out. Creating patriots out of
volunteers. Creating the people as victims
and refugees. Thousands of speakers gather between
the microphone cables heading for electricity. The gentlemen
don't know the meaning of chicken and cow. Merapi
vomits Jakarta, colored very straight.
A lining up that's very straight measures the lava. The gentlemen
of parliament are resting in Germany, using up
their year-end budgets. The ladies are busy
with the state income and expense
budgets for the coming year.

Gentlemen and ladies, Merapi vomits
Jakarta, rife with the seismograph's black lines.
Rivers grow, mountains and islands are
recreated between the airplanes
flying between cities. 28,000 feet above sea
level. The new generation splatters out from electric
scriptures that store their faces. Merapi
is eating dinner in your mouth. At every moment
the TV erupts, shoots out cold lava, cracking every mountaintop
in half. Please, take a photo. Glass
dust splatters out from your eyes, you gentlemen
busy shredding this nation to pieces.

Shit, the land of an us is the land of a we
and the land of a them. Come closer, over here, even
closer, listen to the sound of the seismograph written

by rain. Come closer, gentlemen and ladies,
this isn't the roar of dust
praying.

This is a flame that's making itself up.

EARS OF REVOLUTION

I'm faithful to you, comrade. Be faithful to me
while eating sate and losing your sate skewers. I'll
be faithful to you, comrade. Look at my wounds,
are you faithful enough to sit and to stand. You're faithful
to me while reminding me to sleep and drink
warm tea on Monday mornings. I see your faith
like the party's fidelity on Sunday holiday.
Be faithful to Monday and to Sunday,
comrade. Be faithful enough to applaud before
my corpse. And scream and shout when the factory
puts out goods and commodities, trucks carry
goods and commodities, stores and shops and homes and houses
carry goods and commodities.

Be faithful when traveling between cities, announcing
changes in the price of pulsa at every moment. Be faithful enough to
forget the smell of the state, like the smell of a thief
hiding in his own home. Comrade, do
you have enough money to steal your fidelity? Don't
trip over your own feet. Don't trip over your
own mouth, comrade. Don't trip, comrade, over
your own eyes. All ears are gathering
here, comrade. Ears of revolution that
read the smell of bananas. And feel it when it's
your mouth your mouth collapses to the soles of your feet.

BIRTHDAY WITH WIANTA

We always have parties with the gods
here. Swim in a language that always says
good morning to the bathroom. Our gods are made
of enzymes and vitamin C. The smell of coffee when our
dad's dead body begins to burn. Our prayers don't cast
aspersions on others. *To the joyous
swimming pool, to the honorable electrical pole*, today
we read aloud the Constitution. 1945 with a state ID card and
a credit card in our hands. The noise of currency from
sundry states, the global gold standard and the global gold standard terrify
our land. We make a carving of the rise and fall
of stock prices. We dance with the gods
here, sing with trees whose roots
break through to recollections of
time and every parting.

To wise and righteous enzymes and vitamin C, to
a bedroom that escapes from a blackout,
today we birthday with our childhoods.
Tomorrow we pick up a guest from Russia, examine
brain vibrations and mask dances. The economy carries on
like a shoe that's been mistaken for the Japanese language
in a restaurant. Tomorrow, we birthday again,
like kids celebrating ... *our nation
is free*. Free to take a holiday from history
and install electrical poles at the bottom of the sea.

THE HUDOQ DANCE OF MATALIBAQ

In the early early morning I cut down the forest with
fire and iron. I dance inside the drone of electric
engines, the sound of the saw and the killers whose
blood is made of oil and sleeping pills. In the early
early morning. In the early early morning tree trunks
spill out of your head and fire bursts out of
your stomach. Logs, in the early early
morning, logs float
along the Mahakam River, hauled by thousands of ships that
come from your stomach. In the early early morning the forest
moves, the forest is dragged the length of the Mahakam
River like dragging thousands of your bodies from
nightmares that come via tomorrow. In the early early
morning, tomorrow never arrives at today.
In the early early morning the river and the forest are like a
battlefield where the killings of the children
of tomorrow and the children of today occur.
The Dayak Hibau children whose poisoned
spears have been exchanged for rupiah bills.
My name is Lung Ding Lung Intan. I'm also
called Daleq Devung and Joan Ping. My father
and my wet nurse are a pair of eagles that
often fly into your head in the early early morning.
Then they dance the Hudoq dance. The dance that
taught me about a cave. A cave in
Matalibaq that not a single one of you can
see or find. A cave where
the forest was born. In the early early morning, thousands of forest
corpses are dragged along the Mahakam River. You fucked
our young girls too, with your penis made of
saws and iron. You stole our youths' hearts
via motorboat. In the early early morning
I take back the Mahakam River like

taking my mother's blanket and I put it back
into the cave. You'll no longer own that
massive river. You'll go blind and your stomach will
turn to stone. In the early early morning I take back
the whole forest and place it in the cave.
You'll no longer own our massive forest. You'll
go blind and your head will turn into
a frying pan. In the early early morning the whole lush
forest comes back. Magnificent trees grow
again, and every saw set to fell them
will shatter. Birds fly all around and every
morning sing of the origins of love. Love is
the singing and dancing of time they say. In the early
early morning the whole river is created anew, where
fish build homes from jewels and the blue
sky that pierces through to the bedrock of your life. A floor
on which the river dozes off and embraces your shadow
cast by the dusk sun. In the early early morning someone
finds love like finding a field of time
you'd abandoned in a cardboard box.

PART 3:
VOICES THAT WALK ON GLASS

VOICES THAT WALK ON GLASS

A morning. A road that goes by and comes back, is a
road. On the outskirts of the word, on the membrane separating
looking glass from mirror. The road to morning. An unrecurring
morning. Made of paper cuttings. Waking a
star. A star in your room.

A star that leaves its light on a blank page.
Not working, it dives intensively into idleness. A star. Not moving.
It revolves above a measuring stick of darkness.
Leaving its galaxy among light and seeing. Momentum
in a telescope's alley. A morning. A morning that goes by,
unable to grasp separation.

A star. A whispering star. Voice caught
in the waves of your history. Waves of dust in the friction
of fire on fire. Your history and a keris stabbing. A shriek from the voices
of freedom and faceless masses. Merchant ships
sinking. Mass graves. A morning. Communication
tools that bring storms of speech. Theories of killing
stored in knife handles.

A star. Light that perpetually wanders in the dark.
Astronomical footprints hidden outside the light. Traversing
streams of gas. Explosions of ice. Explosions of dust behind the hush
of a blank page. Love that goes and comes back with voices on
a mirror.

Field of darkness. Black orbits. A star.
A star that takes its own life. Among the hush of
neutrons and protons that keep watch over silence. Among the morning
that's almost morning again. A humanity on the edge of its own shadow.

Hushed. Alone with the alone.
Nearly there, what goes by and comes back
nearly here.

THE PROJECT OF ABORTING ME

Through a long kiss I go flying
down and float down to a burrow that
voids everything about my birthday
between my two thighs. A mystery from you to me
that invents night inside our embrace. I enter
through the tip of your tongue, everything about dreams beside
sleep. And printing machines rain from the south
wind. Memories that void everything about
compositions of recollection.

I go from the bedroom to the living room through
my mother's clothes, floating in front of a photo of my father. My
mother's breath voids everything about the photo of my father. I go
leaving me in the backyard.
Through experiences about picking up
and about boredom. All performances
about me are watched by dead people. Voiding
my body comes back as raw meat. Through
tailors, voiding my clothes, a washing machine, and
a hospital.

Freedom to void myself from the sum of
citizens and anthropological calculations. A boring
book about dying. Through my mother's clothes
re-voiding menstrual blood. Nearing
and obscuring the border between me and me, shooting
my forehead with my blood type. I void
standing and void walking. The story on the dinner
table floats off, challenging the story on the
bed.

The electricity's gone out, aborting all space in
the house and the borders of the regions of difference. A dead

person and a dead person turn on an electric lamp amidst a field of stars.

DEAD MAN EPIDEMIC

Morning, like a time epidemic. I want
to repeat yesterday's morning again. Same sun,
same street cleaners, same coffee sellers at
the coffee shop. Morning, all is not the same
as yesterday again. My blood organizes its cells again,
waking all the creatures lodging
in my body. They're celebrating the morning epidemic.
Warm sunlight, warm coffee, warm fried
bananas. Reminiscences of lovemaking left over
in broken egg shells.

Morning spreads contagiously, until it's like I'm bathing
my own corpse in the bathroom. I clean my teeth,
fingernails, and all of my body that's no longer living,
that's no longer me, that's no longer a morninger.
I celebrate the dead man in a market that burnt
down in Surabaya. Now there's a mall standing
there. A mall with the lingering scent of burnt rice still
stored in its walls.

A double espresso, I order strong coffee. A dead
man hugs me. My darling, he says, I can't
remember you anymore. But I'll never
forget your embrace. Traces of sand on his lips, a
boat that no longer feels time. A
beach that's gone, leaving a grain of sand in
my palm.

A STREET TO FALL ON

You sit your heart down inside the plastic bag on my
desk chair, sit down to light up a poem. Scent of
plastic and corpse perfume. A rainy season so
warm and so January. You sit me down,
the one who's standing on my desk chair, standing to see
what keeps falling. Towards what's lying around
and what's floating away. Towards what's running after
the fall of all I don't need to own.

MUSEUM OF POEMS FROM THE MISSING

My characters this time are a bread entrepreneur, a snail shell,
and an English language store that's
being painted. A woman often comes to the snail
shell, speaking of love, water
boilers, house fencing: everything that's ever more a hassle
to be called human, with lots of commas. I'm
in the middle of the hunt for millions of chickens, to be fed
to the city's population each day, as background information.
A scene outside the gravity of narrative and news.

The English store has been colored red,
this afternoon.

"I found myself inside my cabinet," a woman
says, one among the crowd, her fingernails
colored green. "What's so funny about that
discovery?" asks the bread entrepreneur. "The paradox of the snail
and the English language," she answers. I see the sentence
like an egg hidden in hot frying
oil. Then salt grains between
slices of shallots. The hunt for millions of chickens
to feed to the city's population, and the English
store is already red again, this afternoon.

The cabinet is empty these days, after the bread entrepreneur
sold all his enterprises: freedom for
wheat fields, stocks, work contracts, and
a sad minimum wage. And choosing poetry to
be able to see the smell of shallots, the pops and crackles of an egg
frying in oil. Women too
hide poetry, in every flow of menstrual
blood that leaves their bodies.
This afternoon a snail left its shell, stared into the dusk, holidayed

in death. A lone composite person. A person that splits itself from emptiness.

PORTRAIT OF A FELLED TREE

I told him, today at 7 in the morning. A
Tuesday with the scent of screwpine leaves. Tomorrow,
Wednesday. Yesterday, the jackfruit tree whose fruit
grew in the hot season had an appointment
to meet Wednesday tomorrow morning. But, my neighbor
says, today's Friday. I don't know if
this is just a matter of a difference in grammar between
me and my neighbor. Of course there's a new tradition
between us, between
humans, like we're using chaos as a
way to arrange ourselves. And to survive something that
doesn't make any sense. For example:

There used to be a family here, says the jackfruit
tree. You can see the remnants of a gas stove,
sand that still holds the smell of your pillow, tears
that bind your books and cause your dreams
to turn into a frame that lets loose a portrait of me
on the edge of a Sunday.

STRATEGY ON A CHAIR

A man occupies a TV station. His dark
gray jacket raises his body to the roof
of night, 3 in the morning. His body like an unopenable
door. Rigid. His bloodstream and his organs
scramble into one, all mixed up:
yielding a new composition about a shadowless
man occupying a
TV station.

The man sits in a chair. His sitting
raises his spine to the roof of night, 3
in the morning. A guava red screen behind him. And
a dark gray jacket that doesn't cast a shadow.
He asks every TV camera to shine
on him. He'd like to transform 3 in the morning into
fidgeting in front of TV cameras.

For 12 hours all media is directed at him. 12 hours
pass, the man's only a seat. I take a
seat. Sit in front of the TV. Witness the man.
A shadowless man.
His eyes aren't seeing eyes. But eyes that
don't want to see. 12 hours pass, I'm only a seat in
front of the TV. The man too is only a seat inside the TV.
I turn off the TV. Take off the dark gray
jacket. Take down the guava red screen.
Put the seat back where it came from.
Put all the TV cameras in the cupboard.
Put all the TV's in the storage shed and
lock it.

I'd like to sleep inside my own shadow. Inside
its dark glow, saltwater in my mouth.

LONELINESS ON THE 5TH FLOOR OF A HOSPITAL

A man stares at me after saying
his prayers. His eyebrows look like he wants
to say something, or am I
making that up? — I go up to him and
I kiss his lips. The human body is sad and
holds the carrion of the past. But, his eyebrows
say, my shoulders hurt and can feel
a kiss from the whole of solitude.

I go back to kissing the man, like tomato juice
that doesn't know why the man prays and
at the same time feels like he's
lying. I embrace that man
on the 5th floor of a hospital. The man
watches an ambulance come and break right
through to his heart. He's not sure if it's
the ambulance or if it's the heart.

And then I jump from the 5th floor of the hospital,
and I see my body float, cigarettes
spilling out of my pockets. I see
silence explode from a nurse's dress, and then
I don't see when suddenly I can't feel
time anymore: god, don't leave loneliness
on its own standing on the 5th floor of a hospital. That
man doesn't know if death is a lie
about time or about love.

The man goes back to staring at me after
saying his silence, and makes a meadow
of stars on the hospital window pane.
His kiss resembled saying something, that silence,
it had never lied to him. I watch the man's

face, like a blanket reeking of medicines.
A rat trap beneath a pillow. And you know,
I'm a prisoner of your wounds.

SERMON BENEATH AN ELECTRIC POLE

I let night build a wooden beam into my backbone.
Wind blows like
a gallows dragging along its own rope. Some guy, after
shutting his car door, runs to an electric pole. The noise of the holes
in his body sounds awful, like a prison cell at
11pm. Why are you outside of the sermon you made up yourself?
Why is there mucus dripping from 11pm?

That man is 11pm leaving behind its own
sermon. Is 11pm barely discovering a nail-sized
hole in its palm, dragging silence
from god's throat which created the 11pm man.
Scrapped barbed wire on his forehead and nicotine stains on his
fingertips. That man cleans out every vagina in order
to find his child, sermons forever closed over
by rain hung from electric poles.

Is it true, god, is it true I can see?
Is it true I can hear? Is it true, god, is it true I'm
standing beneath this electrical pole? Is it true I've
replaced a sermon with my own death, not with
someone else's? Is it true I'm proceeding
to leave you behind, to leave my clothes in the car?
Is it true my body has become the church floor?

THE SECRET OF THE LEAK

I'm sweeping the roof tiles while searching for the leak's
secret. A hole either where I'm standing
or around my bed pillow or around my balance searching
for a place to sit down. Dry leaves and volcanic ash
stick to the tiles. There's a bamboo
stalk. A flamboyant tree forcing its growth on
the mossy tiles. Everything will return to green
moss. Not black moss. I'm sweeping the roof tiles.

The moss tells me about the leak in the putty, the
tile paint, the cement and rebar that composes
the sky above our heads. Moss ... eh, how odd it feels
to be human. How busy it feels to be
human. I'm sweeping the roof tiles while
continuing the search for the leak's secret, around the bucket, a hole
in the mop and in the dripping water.

A hole in the dripping water, it says.
Everything will prostrate itself within moss. To the
roof tiles, to the flamboyant flowers
strewn about, I kneel down. Surrendering myself
to the uncalculated. Surrendering myself to
the unnamed. Surrendering myself to all
that refuses to be worshipped, I kneel down.
Let the fire forget my kidneys and bile.
Let the fire forget the clothes on my body.

I sweep 5 in the afternoon from the leak's secret, a
hole in the sunlight that thins out and
crusts over before the borders of night. Before the borders
of the hole whisper away their fundamentals. Before everything
that drips begins to hang from our necks.

A SEA FOR FITRI

I'm not sure which of the waves makes it more the
sea, after your guitar picking. I'm crawling
between a bottle of beer and your heartbeat. I want
to say sea with a capital letter in front.
But I sink under its weight. And I
want to say it again, *sea* ... with letters
that aren't the names of our city's streets. That can
hear your heart as faint as betadine on your wounds.

I'm not sure which of the waves has made it more
the sand, after the wind carries them from
your heart. And I say it, sand ... like the thousands
of periods you've carried from each sentence, gathered
here. Makes it hard for us to trust our legs to stand.
Sitting that doesn't sleep, looking that doesn't
see, a body searches for sand in its
openings.

Reptiles, mammals, amoebas on our tropical skin.
The city's plan builds a stage for performance, humid
afternoon air that makes it possible for me
to embrace your breath, already the sea. Wind, from there
and from here, plays faint changes —
because leaves stir on their branches. Lighting
embers beneath the grilled corn's husks.

Salt air makes us want to cry,
coming in from behind our backs, unexpected
and unexpectable. There and here, birds
with their flying. All at once no longer longing
to go to and fro, like a union of sand not
bound to the sum of its parts. We wonder why we're
able to make stories, and anxious about how I'm

not my sea how I'm not my sky, between
the smell of fish and birds that bear
dusk from the east.

Which is more the sea, what's before us or behind us,
if we go home or if we go out, it's already the sea. Skin
too thin to protect our bodies, to not
sound loudly on the wind and chunks of coral.
On the water beneath our eyelids. Which is dusk. Which
is a bird. Which is a bottle of beer. Which waits for a taxi in front
of the restaurant. Which writes like burying a hole in
the sea.

IN LINE FOR MONEY AT THE BANK

Someone comes and meets my back.
Says something, counts something,
like a burning mattress floating away on a river.
Then he puts an ice cube in my mineral water.

GLOOMY SUNDAY

A suicide song from Hungary, "Gloomy Sunday,"
makes Sunday from my last clothes. A black
full moon wakes me, a house of
clouds and and blood stains on my haircomb. My fingernails
still hold the scent of time. Thoughts that
crash onto a wooden chair. A blanket runs me to
the nest of a nation that forgets the means to make
Sunday.

At twilight on that May Sunday, I felt
time like a world banging on my room.
Newspaper graves, holy books that bleed, and a jungle's
carcass in parliament. I give my heart back to
the sun, I give my life back to the end where the rainbow
takes off its colors. I give it back
like an explosion in a field of stars.

A little bell sounds around my neck, embracing that
melancholy Sunday, *gloomy, gloomy* ... electric cables
have become Sunday on the outskirts of the city. The names
of cities on the final flight are no longer legible.
Stars explode inside a submarine. *Gloomy*
... gloomy ... a dog leads me, Sunday
at the bottom of the sea.

ACROSS FROM A LEAF

I'm not all the leaves on this tree. I'm only
a leaf on this tree. Only this tree and
only a leaf. I'm only a leaf
growing on my neck. Only green like
a leaf. I'm only a leaf that
speaks with my mouth. I mean,
my mouth is a leaf that speaks
with my mouth. I mean, I'm only
a leaf that's a leaf. Don't sweet talk me
into being a tree even though you give me
god. Don't sweet talk me into being all the leaves
on this tree even though you give me the promise
of death. I'm not death's problem or god's problem. I'm
similar, I mean similar to a question I live
not for all the things you say after
death. After death I'm not life and
death is not a leaf that represents all
the leaves on this tree.

I'm only a green color on a tree
I don't know the name of. A tree that makes me
know I'm here, alive here. I mean,
don't scare me like the kids that
run across from death. I remember them
from time to time, and, look over there, look
at the people walking with their legs, trees
growing, children playing joyfully
having a laugh, sky made of a woman's
hair. I am a leaf sewn
onto a tree branch.

LURING SEVEN BUTTERFLIES

I don't go around with eyes wide open. You leave with sleepy
eyes. People here bear a heavy burden. It's not a matter of seeing.
Inside, the burden's full of garbage. Not leaving and sleep-deprivation. We're
busy looking for somewhere to toss all that garbage so we can fill it
again with garbage. You leave with sleepy eyes. I don't go around
with eyes wide open and don't measure what's visible.
You practice yoga and transform into seven butterflies. I watch you
fly and can't follow you in to your butterflies. A circumstance
like solid gas inside an icebox. But there's no explosion.
I don't hear the sound of explosions in this poem. Here life
gets easy, because obviously life's gone. Turned
true by its falseness. Turned beautiful by
its damage. I'm inside your embrace and outside
your flight. Imagining seven butterflies beginning to sow
their wings and sow their flight. Replacing primary earth
with the Marne River's route, which splits your dreams in two.

LUBLINSKIE'S BODY IN A BLACK ICE ALLEYWAY
for gas

The summer goes for a stroll outside your clothes.
From all the compacted reds.
Clothes with stitching of fear
and sadness. The black ice alleyway of the Jews' flight
from Grodzka, become a tourist street.
The summer still stitches up the drizzle,
every window of weather opened and closed.
Not about what's locked out or locked in.
About your lips
leaving a clove seed on my tongue.
Whispering Wislawa Szymborska's poems,
with the suitcase constantly collecting our shadows
from behind. Not breaking apart the sentence with commas,
after the past and the present.
We borrow a bird's wings to no longer
use language like humans.
We fly.
As if in a space outside the temperatures of death.
As if the sun offers illusions of shadows,
and a bus brings night to Warsaw.

Night continuously renovated under the sad
streetlights.
Shifts the summer to the stairway towards
castles of silence,
cafes hiding the cries
of wounded throats.
Men's eyes in plastic bags
begin to swarm the city's parks.

The waiter brings menus of history,
a cup of coffee and ice cream about us.

War history paintings and iron keys
at the Lublinskie Museum.
We go out in a city that's become
a page of the dinner menu.

The rumble of airplanes and trains still renovates
our embrace, among passports, travel maps, and old
churches. I don't know the difference anymore between
a caress and kneeling in prayer before your sadness.
In my suitcase there's still a casket asking for a visa
for the freedom to breathe.

My love, sleep can't paint our dreams.
Lublin's become a silent piano outside night.

WIND BENEATH AN EAR

He's outside of a human kingdom's
dinner. These days, living behind a death.
He dissolves into a glass of wine outside of a human
kingdom's dinner. Wine a
hermit drinks. The glass's lip still
holds the ashes of his cremated body. The scent of wine
reaches a woman knitting
a map over there. *My god,* his voice
like a stretch of valley in the woman's ear.
The scent of wine is the scent of her beloved. And the map
falls from her hands, becoming cities of the voyage.
From Paris to Banten, city of belinjo crackers and the rubble
of spice trade debris. She envisions a long
voyage in those cities, seeking her lover.
With each whiff of wine it's as if she's discovering her lover's
address. But her beloved lies down in
a hermit's belly. She explores those cities,
as if exploring her own knitting.

Each city is like coming back to
the same place. A place where her knitting's strands
unravel, loosed from their mesh. Making an equal
line from the loss behind her. An equal
departure, causing sorrow to shut over her beloved's
address. "*Where is he?*" always becomes
a shadow of "*who am I?*" The scent of wine is
the scent of her lover's corpse. The scent of a hermit's belly.
Is love perhaps, is living perhaps
death's shadow releasing
the knots of yarn from the map
she's knit? She doesn't leave. She returns. She doesn't
go home. She disappears.
She meets the hermit at the border between going home and

disappearing. She undresses: inhales the mouth
of the hermit. She
takes her lover out from the hermit's belly.
A dead soul that makes identical lines at every city's
borders. A soul that doesn't
step on its own shadow.

GUEST OF A TIME

Time's movement is slowing here. It's like I'm
waiting for someone to either open the door or
make the door. I can see my breath moving
and my breath inhales fresh air in the yard
in front of time slowing here. But I'm no
longer here and time is no longer moving slowly.
I'm in front of the entrance to the international airport
which is still closed at 3am not here. Time goes back
to slowing down and I go back to being here,
without the international airport at 3am. I can
see my breath moving to gather my earlier
breath which was made between either slow
time or fast time.

I'm here and then I go out to the street that's
no longer here. Here I no longer see
when I go out to the street that's no longer
here. Why do I go out and see here
no longer. Now I'm approached by a cat of
a cat that earlier didn't approach and wasn't here
before. That cat, its eyes are like a boar that
wants to take out my intestines and why am I thinking
as if seeing an action that isn't
enacted, and making time even
slower.

I'm already not here, now, here, when time rotates
again to the number 2 after the number 2
it passes by. But I'm still here and the number 2 isn't
going anywhere. Here, where time
makes my body into a cross here,
with a face bowing down to the dirt, yet
looking up to the dirt.

— I've already been now.

INDEX

And walking. And sleeping. And forgetting. And sweeping. And eating. And picking up the laundry. And photographing someone else's wedding in a cafe in Shanghai. And reading. And cutting your nails. And photographing cat sex at Lely's house. And visiting my friend's grave in Surabaya. And his kid's in college. And his kid sends a text, who is my father? And his kid doesn't sleep in her mother's room. And her name is Dya Ginting. And burning the trash. And mowing the lawn. And picking up a plastic bag that somebody threw to the curb. And kissing a puppy. And visiting a friend who's crying at his laptop. And wanting to live in Maria Callas' voice. And not having money. And waiting for royalties from poetry. And meeting Caligula's corpse in language. And bathing. And wanting to say to you that I've already said it.

AFTERWORD: NOTES BENEATH SHADOWS

A hard, driving rain. Needling drops of water drip over and over again, constantly, evenly, in layers, making drapes of water, shining, bunched tightly together, over and over, constantly, falling, in layers, broken but continuous, faint but densely arrayed, streaks criss-crossing vertically and horizontally, shining, quivering in sweeps of wind. I feel like copying and pasting this sentence over and over here, so that this writing drops like rain as it fills up the pages. A sentence forced into writing, from the awareness I've held all along that I'll never be able to encounter the rain through writing.

The perpetual repetition of the lines of rain causes space to continually transform, while simultaneously immortalizing space. That constant repetition makes it seem precisely as if the rain water was suspended in the air, rather than falling. An architecture active outside of construction, merely following gravity's law to fall over and over again. Not engendering a presence that goes by and is exchanged again for another. A repetition that doesn't give rise to time and sound. Time just barely occurs when the rain begins to come down, touching forms, touching the ground: leaving behind an uneven wetness, uneven puddles, elsewhere maybe leaving behind a flood. Even sound just barely occurs when the rain begins to fall, touching forms. A varied and disparate sound, due to the differences in the forms' materials. The rain's fall over forms is a harsh collision between liquids and solids. The intensity of the rain is represented by the sound volume of this collision's harshness.

The crash of rainwater sounds like it'll smash through the roof. Below that roof, I'm trying to sleep. The room is besieged by the sound of rain. A sound I can't touch. But my ears go on recording the siege of that sound. A sound that creates new walls, removes and replaces the whole construction of the room. Transforms the whole structure of the room into the structure of the sound. But I'm not wet, though there's a leak in the roof. I'm not under the rain, but I am under the siege of the rain's sound. Fingers clenched. Renewing and returning the fearful trembling I feel faced with something outside myself. Terrifying.

The repetition of the rain-sound's siege carries on as if taking apart a piece of myself, making renovations to the space within me. The sound of the rain results in the opening of an unmeasurable and invisible internal space. It's as if I'm present in an untallied inside-myself within that internal space. The leaking roof and the rainwater constantly dripping to the floor begin to make a puddle, actually returning to the constitution of the room's construction: that I'm there in the leaking room. The leakage accordingly seeps into my internal space and accompanies the development of a solitude not limited by sadness. I feel like copying and pasting this part of the paragraph over and over here, so that this writing can show how the sound of the rain makes renovations to my internal space as it fills up its pages. A sentence forced into writing, from the awareness I've held all along that I'll never be able to encounter the sound of the rain through writing.

In that case, so, it follows that, therefore, is, but, maybe, could be, for a time, perhaps ... *is that writing?*

The rain constitutes a personification of myself in writing, a personification of nature-I by way of a collision within culture-I. The struggle between nature-I and culture-I is constant, due to the presence of unexpected factors that come by way of the "birth" and "death" that take place in the middle of cultural management. In order to prevent us from realizing that we live in an obsolete and weathered era, culture possesses a mechanism to continuously revamp and renew itself within its obsolescence and frailty. Steadily renovating the past in order to multiply the space of the present as a time industry. Birth and death exist outside of culture. Consequently each religion makes up various myths in order to seize birth and death as fields for dogma-theology. Exploiting them as grand narratives and institutionalizing them as divine revelation.

Writing as a failure of which we've been conscious from the start isn't my choice. The fact is that I can't write as a first person. The first person (I) is already gone by the time it writes. Writing is done by changing the first person (I) into the third person (them). I can't write I in a time and place that coincide: the camera can't take a picture of the camera, my eyes can't look out and see me. Writing occurs just after I elapse, becoming them. A reading like this is, for me, important in understanding my position as an installation of an I that's already passed, understanding space as a representation of the passage of time and I perpetually within its simultaneity. A passage that's institutionalized through language's grammar. But language itself isn't a representation of simultaneity. Each word in a sentence must be aligned within the linear laws of language.

Writing as a "fundamental separation from I," a killing of oneself as a first person, and then I begin to become conscious of it as a healing of existential wounds, akin to what my generation experienced earlier. Existential wounds that are tangible in our relations with the world around us, social life, family, education, work, love, economy, politics, even religion. Life as a poet is tantamount to creating poverty. A poverty that occasionally has far-reaching results, takes part in damaging the conception of my self in public space. And, conversely, this poverty also takes part in creating my internal space: there are no banks or insurance companies in my internal space. In writing, the death of the first person and the birth of the third person produce a kind of new body. A body similar to how I depicted the rain at the beginning of this writing. A body that isn't present in the rain, but is present in the rain-sound's siege, with its curtains of sound and leaking roof. A new body that arrives through the reversed path from death (I) to birth (them). I wrote the poems in this collection in an atmosphere like what's described above. An atmosphere of the mind's pressure where I let the currents of drowning-I enter. The desire to kill myself that almost always comes together with the fear of doing it. To do it or not, turns out just the same. Within those currents of drowning-I, the suicide's already happened. A constant suicide of external-I's dying in order to exist and to reassemble within internal-I.

Who is this external-I? In the last 20 years, we've entered communal life into a socialization of space as a product of the reproduction of previously unimaginable softwares. 24 hours a day, the world community can produce new spaces via the internet. The borders between East and West have thawed through a variety of identity migration phenomena. 20 years colored by numerous changes related to the ways we view our human culture and identity: DNA research, international financial control, the aggression of urban subcultures, a variety of technological innovations that can be used by the general populace such as GPS and ATM machines, world population problems, and the threat of food crises.

These external conditions, often referred to as a "soft-power war," form a great river whose delta floods into each individual's internal life. Concepts of space and time are undergoing changes that are no longer framed by an understanding of how communities of times past were required to forfeit their reproductive space. We're required to live in a space dump as commodity, with time as a memory control experienced by contemporary society. Contemporary art, increasingly tending toward plastic arts, is developing as if viewing the world as a warehouse rearranged beneath the reek of used goods, meat taken out of the freezer, stories taken out from the coffin of media politics, light exploited to isolate the light source. Transforming materials into media. The flow of culture's externalization carries on with increasing power. External-I grows bigger, leaving internal-I in its fields of silence.

I have copy-pasted the two paragraphs above into several of my writings. They originally come from a curatorial essay that Carolyn Christov-Bakargiev wrote for the Documenta (13) exhibition in Kassel, Germany, 2012 ("The dance was very frenetic, lively, rattling, clanging, rolling, contorted, and lasted for a long time"). I experienced Carolyn's essay, along with the Documenta (13) exhibition, like an earthquake that clogged up my poetry. An exhibition in which the revocation of the limits of art was achieved via a leakage of space, a broadening of narration, and an imagining through design.

After attending that exhibition, I felt like ending all the poems in this collection. Poems that, for the most part, I'd like to call "installations of emptiness." Knit from meaningless matters. Emptiness like rain that goes on and on, over and over again, but loses its gravity. Loses the construction that can knit it all together. Relations vulnerable to my surroundings, that all too easily come undone or change position, losing their binding link, occurring so effortlessly and still leaving their wounds inside. A vulnerability that also occurs in memories, readings, and public appreciations for our common life. The political culture in Indonesian sinks deeper and deeper by letting money and power extend further as the primary links of sociality among communities as well as individuals.

I've lost the structure on which to establish myself or to be established. I've lost interest in "establishing myself" within the phenomena of fragmented-I, as described above. Letting fragmented-I and drowning-I be is tantamount to letting poetry act as an anti-structure. The only blueprint by which I'm able to regain the structure of poetry is language. But I don't want to go back to depending on language, or using language as poetry's identity; particularly in the context of Indonesia, where many poets live with a different mother tongue than the language they use day-to-day. Poetry, though it uses language, is not a product of language. The rhyming games played through the sounds of language in classical poetry presuppose the power structure between the poet within the palace walls and the power within language itself. Lyric-I can't be returned to a poetic space like this through language, because the space of its reproduction clearly no longer exists. Returning to a poetic space like this tends to be a return to the salonization of language. The trouble of positioning time and history within language. I see poetry more as a work of art than a work of literature.

Actually, I'm unwilling to replace rain with language. Though I'll never be able to write rain.

I've done much work in the triangle between language, the body, and space. I'm still trying to believe: the body should create and forever renew language through day-to-day experience, wonder, the arrival of questions that celebrate uncertainty. But the reality I face is that language is a monster that generates communication in order to make-gone-by events and make-gone-by me. Language gives rise to illusions about me. Language negates the simultaneous relations between my body and the space outside my body. Language makes me into the external-I that keeps going by, cancelling the me that came before. Language creates linear time through its grammar. I need some kind of wall within language, so as to look at and contemplate language.

The biggest push to treat language as my body comes as a result of the fact that I can't be outside of space and time. Space and time always present a surface: where the tireless negotiation between the space outside me and the space within me occurs. An externalizing process that takes place through language and culture, giving rise to the meta-narrative between external-I and internal-I. I can't accept a culture-I that turns dogmatic toward nature-I.

Language, the body, and space form a continuously arriving triangle, latent, that fascinates my observation like a laboratory of darkness in various acts of viewing: can my eyes see into me?

In this triangle between language, the body, and space, the poems in this collection are like a piece of knitting that leaves its unknit leftover strands among the triangle's shadows: language-shadow, body-shadow, and space-shadow. Sometimes I want to write poetry anti-poetically: leave the dimensions unbound, reality discontinuous, memories unarchived in order to discover their own distinct skies.

The conditions of Indonesia's political culture are anti-meaning; having lost their dedication, having lost the meaning of nation and state, they produce words of aggression that are broadcast over and over again on TV, and plunge their virus in to damage the distance needed to consider something. The triangle between language, the body, and space exists in the push and pull between how poetry is practiced as language and how politics is practiced as a destroyer of meaning. The poems in this collection don't want to be caught in the latent trap produced by this push and pull. The closest position I can take is to trust in my body, to listen to it, and to rediscover the fact of myself as nature-I. Nature-I that opens itself further in considering the multiplicity of me, the fragility, the instincts of life and death outside of the value externalizing process performed by exterior discourse authorities.

The poetry that I write is more like the emptying of various documentations from my body, in the hope that the body remains present as the original fact of nature-I: a suitcase constantly filled to be emptied again, so that shadows remain alive. An emptying of documentation for how poetry continues to hold space in the building of shadow bridges between positions of time, space, even the market's aggressions that commodify worth. Waiting for the permanent openness of the space of possibility to step back from culture.

The I that's lost the structure needed to return to "standing myself up" I experience as a permission to reaccept the presence of silence. I grant an expanded space to the presence of silence. Let silence carry away the definitive burdens around my understanding of myself as someone. Reconnect my body with the matters closest at hand, my body with my dogs, with the objects around me, plants, buildings, housework that has to be done. A body as a body, instead of a body as someone. The silence sometimes becomes too powerful, carrying away my whole self; turning silence itself into a museum of I. The effort to release my body from its understanding of itself as someone causes me to consistently step back into silence.

A few times I've come across people I know, friends, on an airplane or somewhere else. I try to hide my face so that I'm not recognized. Dodge the possibility of meeting. It's like I'm steadily stepping backwards into becoming a mute. Entering my internal hollow. A storehouse dense with shadows of silence. Driving away every desire to experience myself as someone. Trying to experience once more the feeling of being alone, of sorrow. Acting to empty, rather than fill. Ceaselessly so, like cleaning a mirror that's already clean.

ACKNOWLEDGMENTS

The translator wishes to thank Afrizal Malna for his trust and encouragement in translating these poems; Nuraini Juliastuti and Andy Fuller for giving them a good home at Reading Sideways Press; Anna Gurton-Wachter, Lelaki Budiman, Lewis Freedman, Mikael Johani, Rebekah Smith, Tiaswening Maharsi, and others for fruitful conversation about the poems and invaluable insight into their translation; and Diyah Noor for immeasurable support, incisive feedback, and good humor throughout.

Earlier iterations of some of these translations appeared in *A Perfect Vacuum, Asymptote, Dispatches from the Poetry Wars, Mekong Review, Reading Sideways Magazine, The Brooklyn Rail,* and *Washington Square Review.* Many thanks to the editors.

Work on this translation was supported by the LitRI Translation Grant from the National Book Committee of Indonesia's Ministry of Education and Culture.

About Afrizal Malna

Afrizal Malna is currently active in the theatre program of the Jakarta Arts Council. His most recent books include Kepada Apakah (2013); Anxiety Myths (trans. Andy Fuller, Lontar, 2013); drucktmaschine drittmensch (a collection of poems translated into German by Urilke Draesner, Katrin Bandel, Sophie Mahakam Anggawi, published by DAAD, Berlin, 2015). Other books include *Berlin Proposal* (Nuansa Cendekia, Bandung 2015); *Teks Cacat di luar Tubuh Aktor* (Kalabuku, Yogyakarta, 2017); *Pada Batas Setiap Masakini* (Octopus, Yogyakarta, 2017). Afrizal has recently been involved in the following events and residencies: DAAD Berlin (2014-15), Poetry on the Road International Bremen (May 2014); Berlin International Literature Festival (September 2014); Maastricht International Poetry Night (October-November 2014); the Litprom Southeast Asia Literature Festival of Frankfurt (January 2015); the International Poetry Festival in Kerala (February 2016); and has participated in the Tokyo Performing Arts Meeting in Yokohama thanks to a grant from the Japan Foundation in 2017.

About Daniel Owen

Daniel Owen is the author of the poetry books *Restaurant Samsara* (Furniture Press, 2018), winner of the 2017 Furniture Press Poetry Prize, and *Toot Sweet* (United Artists Books, 2015), and the chapbook *Authentic Other Landscape* (Diez, 2013). From 2009 to 2014 he co-edited and produced the poetry zines *Sun's Skeleton and Poems by Sunday*. Recent writing has been published in *Counter, Hyperallergic, Vestiges*, and *The Recluse*.

Since 2012 he has worked with the Brooklyn-based publishing collective Ugly Duckling Presse and has edited and designed various and sundry books for UDP, including Mirtha Dermisache's *Selected Writings* (co-published with Siglio Press), Hirato Renkichi's *Spiral Staircase* (translated by Sho Sugita), and Jacqueline Water's *Commodore*, among many others. He currently serves as UDP's Publicity Director.

Daniel's translations of poems by Afrizal Malna won Asymptote Journal's 2019 Close Approximations Translation Contest and have been published in *Mekong Review, The Brooklyn Rail, A Perfect Vacuum, Washington Square Review*, and *Dispatches*.

About Reading Sideways Press

Reading Sideways Press is a Melbourne-based small press founded by Nuraini Juliastuti and Andy Fuller. Reading Sideways Press publishes books and zines on art, sports and literature.

www.ingramcontent.com/pod-product-compliance
Lightning Source LLC
Chambersburg PA
CBHW051953290426
44110CB00015B/2222